Who's Driving the Bus?

A storybook for grown-ups and those who are mostly so

By Linda Graves

Illustrations by Gerald Barlow

Books Academy LLC
112 SW H K Dodgen Loop,
Temple, Texas 76504
Hotline: (254) 800-1189

Ordering Information:
Quantity sales. Special discounts are available on quantity purchases by corporations, associations, and others. For details, contact the publisher at the address above.

Printed in the United States of America.

ISBN-13:   Softcover   978-1-964929-63-7
           eBook   978-1-964929-64-4

Library of Congress Control Number: 2024921871

Dedication

Who's Driving the Bus?

This book is dedicated to my children, biological and "adopted". I love you for the challenges and joy you bring to my life. My prayer is that you will always let Jesus drive.

Acknowledgements:

To those have assisted me with editing and comments regarding Who's Driving the Bus? I want to thank you. That includes the deaconesses of Community Covenant Church in Rocklin, California, my mentor and my spiritual growth partner for a few years, Lois Solberg, and my brother, Bob Lambert. I want to thank my brother-in-law, Jerry Barlow, who drew the illustrations at my request from the goodness of his heart.

To Lowell, my chief encourager of 52 years, who thinks I can do anything I set my mind to doing, how I appreciate you!

And to the Holy Spirit, who gave me the idea in one giant flash early one morning while I was in a rehab center after having a knee replaced, I am so grateful that You chose me as the vessel with which to carry this message.

Who's Driving the Bus?

A story book for grown-ups and those who are mostly so.

Everyone has a bus. Buses have seats—some more seats, some less, but all buses have seats. Some also have compartments where things are stored, where attitudes reside, where our story is kept. Where is your story kept?

Draw a picture of those places here:

When we are young, someone else is in charge of our bus, but as we get older, we start to take over command of the bus. We share that control with parents or other adults throughout childhood, preteen, and teen years. Sometimes we don't like the way others control our bus. We learn ideas, behaviors, morals, guidelines, and how to live from those who drive our bus.

Write or draw some things that you learned from those whos drove your bus.

As we grow older, we gain authority regarding our bus, where it travels, who is on it, how fast it goes, what passengers and cargo it carries, and its destinations.

What direction would you like your bus to go?

We like to be in charge of driving the bus, make the decisions, be in control, and be in charge. We have passengers on our bus—some invited, some not. Some we invite in, and others come through the back door, with or without our knowledge.

The passengers vary. Some passengers are characters like Envy, Jealousy, Hatred, Self-Centeredness. Patience, Kindness, Meekness, and Self-Control might be on the bus. There's Ambition, Fear, Desire, Anger, Retribution, Independence on some buses.

There are Circumstances, Talents, and Skills. There are Success and Failure, nicknamed Winner and Loser, respectively. Family history, Addictions, Co-Dependence, Depression, and Suicidal Thoughts can also have a seat on the bus.

Some passengers are wolves in sheep's clothing, disguised so that our eyes are blinded to what or who is hiding underneath.

Name or draw the characters on your bus.

We grow confident in driving our bus, being in charge. After all, we are adults. We can make our own decisions, choose our own destiny.

Life gets busy. We get overly confident. We got this thing called "life" down pat. Life is good. It has its ups and downs, but overall, life is good.

Our bus might hum along, maybe for years, with everything just as we think it should be. The road is not too hard, the mountains are not too steep, the bridges are a little scary but passable. All is well. The passengers are a little rowdy and sometimes disruptive, but we can handle it. We mature. Life throws us a curve ball now and again, but usually we handle it just fine.

Draw pictures to represent those "curve balls" that you have had to handle.

Then we wake up and realize we have been on the wrong road. The bus is not going to the destination we thought. Someone else got the big promotion. We lose our job altogether. Or we get the new promotion, and it is an awful position, full of deceit and moral values that we can't live with, but we have to, because we have worked for a lifetime to be here, sacrificing and planning, passing up other opportunities that didn't look as good.

Many of the characters on the bus are SHOUTING, loud, raucous, so loud one cannot hear to think. There is a cacophony of noise, each trying to rise over the others, to be in control. Some voices are quiet, too quiet to hear. One would not even know that they are even on the bus. A glance in the rearview mirror, and we see that there are passengers on the bus that we don't remember letting on. How did that character get on the bus? Who let him in? And there's so many. Who are all those characters? They are so distracting, trying to get me to go here, take that road, and go over there.

Who do you see when you look in the rearview mirror? Where are they trying to get you to go?

They are fussing, complaining, whispering, shouting, wrestling, and even tickling. The road looks unsafe. Busyness everywhere. It stresses me out.

The noise. The distraction. The busyness. Work. Time with family. Demands. Not enough time. I would like some leisure time. Some fun. There's not time. There's no money. Too many demands. If I am going to keep my job, I must spend more effort, work harder. The kids need my attention. My spouse is saying, "I need more attention!" I don't have time to do an inventory to see if I am doing what is best.

Make your "to-do" list here. Use all the space you need. Add a page if necessary

One of the devious passengers has subtly wrapped long, bony fingers around my leg, choking the blood supply, and now my foot is going numb. There are periods where things are better, but then they worsen again. I am just not doing that well overall. I am not making good progress.

I am lost. The road is treacherous and much too narrow for a bus, and the pavement is non-existent. How did life get this difficult? This complicated? There is nowhere to turn around.

Others want to drive. Envy has slithered to the front and is crawling up my back, soon to wrap itself around my arms and heart, and next thing I know, it has control of the wheel. I am possessed by wishing I were living someone else's life, someone without all this mess.

I am ambivalent, but relieved, to not have to make all those decisions as I relinquish the wheel to Envy. It doesn't take long to figure out that we REALLY are on the wrong road now. In BIG trouble. Eventually, I have control of the bus. I hear a constant drone: "Why can't you have what your friends have? Are you being punished? You're obviously not as good as they are. Why don't you make more money?

Why can't you buy that present that you want? All your friends have one. You must not be as good as they are!" And on and on it goes.

The bus is too long to negotiate the turns and must back up to the edge of the cliff to get around. The wheel scrunches on the gravel as the tire slips over the edge. But the driver, currently me, revs the engine, and the bus groans as it rights itself on the narrow road.

It's musical chairs. Sometimes I am in the driver's seat with Compassion right behind me. But in a flash, Compassion can be replaced by Jealousy. Hatred is usually in the back but, on occasion, makes his way to the front to whisper in my ear. I like Wisdom and Discernment, but I can't even find them in all the chaos on the bus.

Who has control of the steering wheel in my life?

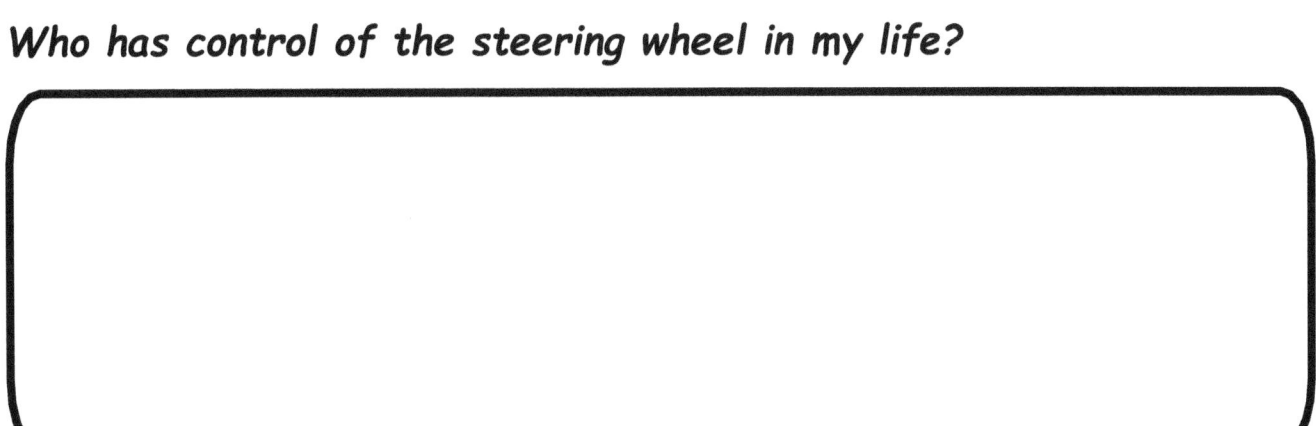

As I gain experience driving the bus, I have time, usually for only moments, to look at who I have allowed on my bus. What a motley crew of characters, ranging from Authority to Zealousness. Some completely evil, some good, and some that can be good or evil. And there is the One who has been relegated to a seat so far away that I cannot see Him in the rearview mirror, and I certainly cannot hear His still, small voice in the chaos of life.

Amidst the chaos, however that looks to every individual, it is difficult to find our peace, our purpose, our meaning. But amid the seats, amid the characters that we have allowed to be on the bus, there is One. Those that are Believers have One who can bring order to the chaos. Can we hear Him through the din? Can we see Him though the faces, the characters?

Self-sufficiency is saying, "You need no one. You can do this yourself."

Pride is shouting, "I will let no one take over. I am all that I need."

False humility is whispering, "I am not good enough to deserve _____."

We fill in the blank.

Work is calling out, "Come, you have much more to do. Do not be distracted. After all, I pay your bills."

The children are crying, "I need you to take care of me.   I want your attention because it means you love me! Don't you love me?"

What are your voices telling you?

```



```

Jealousy is subtle. Not shouting out but surreptitiously winding tentacles around my heart and mind, whispering evil thoughts, devious thoughts of deserving of what others have. After all, I am just as good, work just as hard or harder than most to follow the rules. I deserve what they have more than they do.

It may take days. It may take months. It may take years. But eventually, for those who are Believers, we see One working His way, sometimes very slowly, up to the front of the bus. We must evict a few characters to make a place for Him. And sometimes we can't get the ones off the bus that are dominating our thoughts and actions. *What dominates your thoughts and actions?*

He sits right behind the driver's seat when He arrives. He leans over and whispers quietly in my heart, "Would you like for me to drive?" "No, that's okay. I've got this." Independence, known as Autonomy, has taken over again. And we struggle on.

But I wear out. I am tired. I get sick. I have more catastrophes, either physically or emotionally. At some point, I relinquish control of the bus. Again. But this time, it is to the One. I need rest.

As we trade seats, I am amazed at the peace that washes over me because nothing has changed yet—except the driver. The change is not necessarily fast. But, over time, one by one, the troublemakers are evicted off the bus.

Some are harder to get rid of than others. They are more tenacious. More conniving. They return again and again, sometimes wearing disguises so that they aren't recognized.

The road is still narrow, rough, and twisting, but the Driver is skilled, negotiating the turns, slowing and speeding up as necessary. He seems to know about the blind corners and when there is an oncoming vehicle. He just knows.

Sometimes new riders get on the bus. Peace replaces Malcontent. Creativity pushes Envy away. Fear is replaced by Confidence, but the confidence is in the Driver, not in me. I remember how I handled the bus. And He talks to me. I rest. I can listen. He offers me assistance to do things, but He doesn't force me. It's my decision. Sometimes I make good ones. Other times not so much.

I'd like to tell you that He always drives my bus, the One who knows the Way, but, unfortunately, that isn't true. Periodically, I take over driving the bus again. But before long, I see that I still don't have the skill that it takes to handle the bus on this road of life. There is only one Driver who is skilled enough to take me safely through to the end. I'd like to take charge, but then I get in trouble again, and in due time, I realize that I am driving the bus again.

So—who is driving your bus?

Who is driving your bus?

┌───┐
│   │
│   │
│   │
└───┘

It's one thing to know Jesus as Savior, to be saved from sin by the blood that Jesus shed for us at the cross of Calvary, but the question is, "Do you know Him as LORD of your life?" When He is LORD, He drives our bus. If you don't know Jesus as LORD, He cannot drive your bus. If you don't know Jesus as LORD, you do not allow Him to drive your bus. So think about it.

Who is driving your bus?

Do you not know? Have you not heard? *The LORD is the everlasting God, the Creator of the ends of the earth. He will not grow tired or weary, and his understanding no one can fathom. He gives strength to the weary and increases power to the weak. Even youths grow tired and weary and young men stumble and fall; but those whose hope is in the LORD will renew their strength. They will soar on wings like eagles; they will run and not grow weary. They will walk and not faint. Isaiah 40:28-31*

And they will allow the One to drive the bus.

Who's Driving the Bus?

Discussion Guide

1. How large is your "bus"?

   ┌───┐
   │   │
   │   │
   └───┘

2. What "compartments" are on your bus?

   ┌───┐
   │   │
   │   │
   └───┘

3. What are some of the "things" that you carry in those compartments?

   ┌───┐
   │   │
   │   │
   └───┘

4.   Who drove your bus when you were unable to drive it yourself?

5.   What ideas, behaviors, morals did you learn from those who drove your bus?

6.   At what age did you start intermittently driving your own bus?

7. What were the results of taking over intermittently from parents or others who drove your bus?

a.   What were the experiences you remember?

b.   What were the outcomes of you driving your bus?

c.   How did you decide what to do in the circumstances where you had control of the choices?

d.   What influenced your decision-making?

8. Do you like making your own decisions, large or small?

9. Who is riding on your bus?

10. Have the characters changed through your lifetime?

11. Who are some of the characters that have shown up that surprised you?

12. Are there any characters that you would have liked to see on the bus but weren't there?

13.   Make a list of the characters that are on your bus now. Beside each one, note whether that character works for good, for evil, or both. Or maybe for neither.

   a.   Put a mark by those characters that have been on your bus since childhood.

14. Are there any characters that made it on the bus disguised as something else, and then you discovered they weren't what they appeared to be?

15. Recall a period of life when you felt in charge and all was going according to plan.

16. Recall a time when you discovered that you were on the "wrong road."

a. What brought you to that conclusion?

b. What did you do about it?

17. What are some of the voices that you hear on your bus?

18. How do you decide which ones to listen to?

19. Have you ever "awakened" to find that you have a "character" in your life that you didn't want, when you thought you'd never "be like that"?

  a. Have you stepped back and said, "Who is that person that I've become?"

  b. What were your thoughts with that revelation?

20. What characters have you allowed to take over your life?

a. At what time?

b. Who takes over now?

c. Did you allow them to take over by omission, you not paying attention, or commission, by your will, (I plan to, I am going to, and nothing's going to stop me!)?

21. Have you driven your bus over the cliff?

   a. How?

   b. And what was the recovery process?

   c. What did you learn?

22. With whom do you currently play musical chairs for the driver's seat?

23. Whose voices constantly distract you?

   a. What are they saying?

   ```
   ┌─────────────────────────────────────┐
   │                                     │
   │                                     │
   │                                     │
   └─────────────────────────────────────┘
   ```

24. Is the Holy Spirit on your bus?

   a. If so, where is He sitting?

   ```
   ┌─────────────────────────────────────┐
   │                                     │
   │                                     │
   │                                     │
   └─────────────────────────────────────┘
   ```

25. What percentage of today has the Holy Spirit driven your bus?

   a) What would it take to make that percentage more?

   ```
   ┌─────────────────────────────────────┐
   │                                     │
   │                                     │
   │                                     │
   └─────────────────────────────────────┘
   ```

26. What do you need to do to allow the Holy Spirit to drive your bus?

27. What characters do we need to get off the bus?

   a. What steps do we take to make that happen?

28. If we are honest, we know that none of us, while on this earth, let the Holy Spirit drive our bus 100 percent of the time.

   a.   What action steps do you need to take to allow the Holy

         Spirit to drive your bus?

   b.   What results do you see if you let the Holy Spirit

         drive the bus more and more?

29. What is the difference between "Savior" and "Lord"?

30. What does "Lord" mean?

31. How do I allow the Holy Spirit to be Lord of my life?

32. How do I keep Him Lord of my life instead of jumping back in the driver's seat?

33. When the Holy Spirit drives the bus, there will be surprises, things I don't plan nor expect. How am I going to respond?

34. How do I keep the Holy Spirit in the driver's seat?

What is your Prayer today?

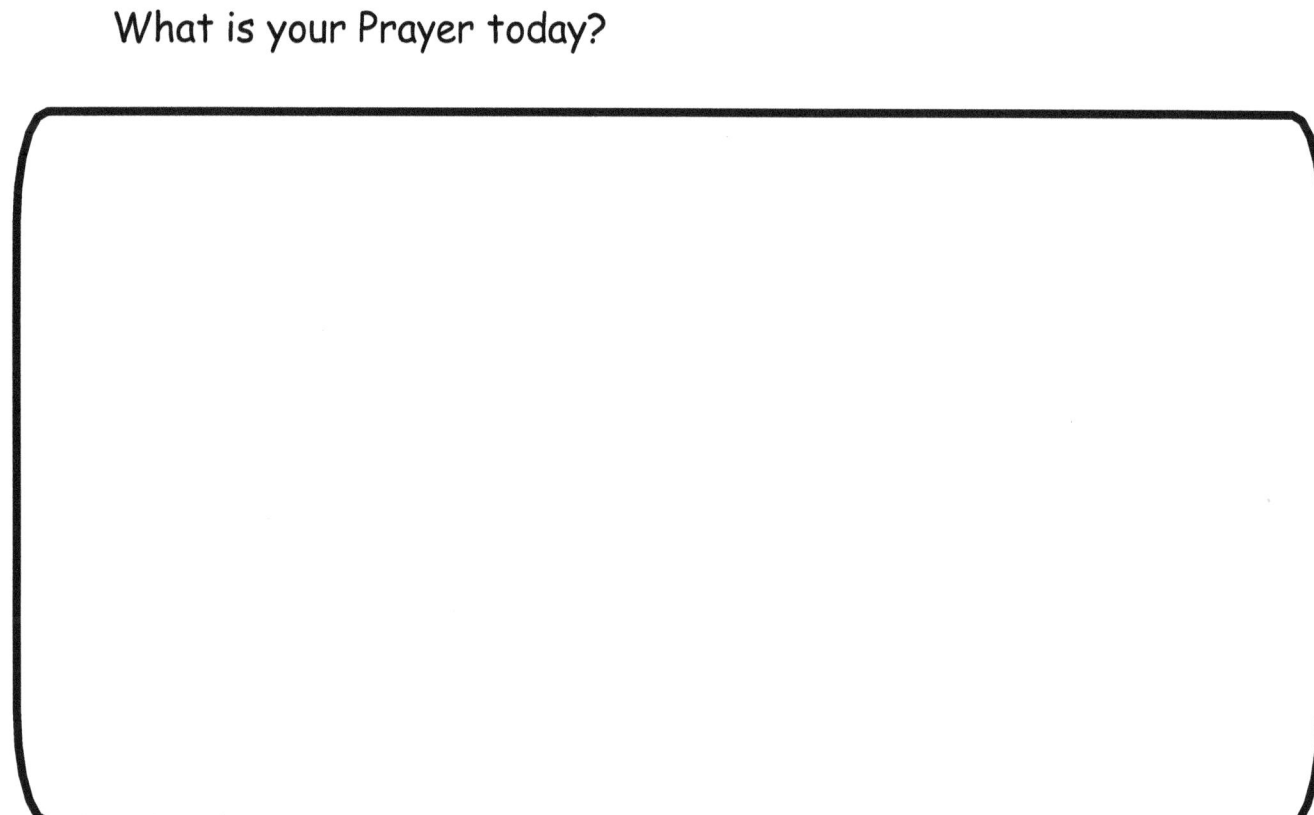

www.ingramcontent.com/pod-product-compliance
Lightning Source LLC
Chambersburg PA
CBHW041155120626
46547CB00020B/3227